THE LOVE LIST

THE LOVE LIST

A Guide to Getting Who You Want

ELENA MURZELLO

iUniverse LLC
Bloomington

THE LOVE LIST
A GUIDE TO GETTING WHO YOU WANT

Copyright © 2011, 2013 Elena Murzello.

All rights reserved. No part of this book may be used or reproduced by any means, graphic, electronic, or mechanical, including photocopying, recording, taping or by any information storage retrieval system without the written permission of the publisher except in the case of brief quotations embodied in critical articles and reviews.

"The Love Puddle" By James Laughlin, from THE SECRET ROOM, copyright ©1997 by James Laughlin. Reprinted by permission of New Directions Publishing Corp.

iUniverse books may be ordered through booksellers or by contacting:

iUniverse
1663 Liberty Drive
Bloomington, IN 47403
www.iuniverse.com
1-800-Authors (1-800-288-4677)

Because of the dynamic nature of the Internet, any web addresses or links contained in this book may have changed since publication and may no longer be valid. The views expressed in this work are solely those of the author and do not necessarily reflect the views of the publisher, and the publisher hereby disclaims any responsibility for them.

Any people depicted in stock imagery provided by Thinkstock are models, and such images are being used for illustrative purposes only.

Certain stock imagery © Thinkstock.

ISBN: 978-1-4917-0071-6 (sc)
ISBN: 978-1-4917-0072-3 (hc)
ISBN: 978-1-4917-0073-0 (e)

Library of Congress Control Number: 2013913284

Printed in the United States of America.

iUniverse rev. date: 9/3/2013

The Love Puddle

is not deep but it's
usually muddy. If you

stray into it you won't
drown but you may come

out of it looking like
a tramp and with your

feelings more dishevel-
led than your trousers.

You may feel guilty or
feel betrayed or even

disgusted, you'll wonder
why you walked through

the love puddle instead
of going around it. But

you know you'll do it
again—that's for sure.

*A poem by James Laughlin (*Secret Rooms: Poems, *1997)*

Contents

Preface ix
Introduction xiii
The Ideal 1
    Why the List? 2
    The List: Help or Hindrance? 3
    Potato Soup versus Lobster Theory 4
    How Does the List Work? 6
The List 9
    Development of the List 9
    The Science behind the List 12
    Women and Mating 13
    Men and Mating 18
    List Gone Wrong 23
Waiting: The Crazy Cat Lady Lingers 29
Master's Degree in Love 41
    Operations—The Process 42
    Strategy, or What's Your Game Plan? 44
    Diversifying Your Portfolio 46

Reallocation of Resources 52
Return on Investment (ROI) 59
Interview Notes 61
Thoughts 69
Shout-Outs 71
References 75

Preface

Okay, here it is. I don't have any writing credits to my name. I somehow coerced my high school English teacher to give me an A during my final semester of school. I think I told her that English was bringing down my GPA and I deserved an A. Not because my writing was stellar or because my well-rehearsed performance of a witch in *Macbeth* was fit for Broadway—I deserved an A because I had heart. I still have heart, and this is why I'm writing this book. I really believe that we live in a time where anything is possible and nothing is too good to be true. And for a non-writer to go on to be a published author is, well, crazy. But we live in a crazy world. Welcome!

I don't think that I'm a guru or that I know it all. What I'm about to tell you is nothing new. In fact, I'm pretty sure you have heard it all before, maybe from your mom or your best friend or a helpful taxi driver. What I'm about to tell you has been rehashed several times over like a well-worn T-shirt that is a snuggly companion as you watch a romantic comedy on a rainy day.

Just so it's clear: this book is based on my real-life experiences and the research I have done through books, articles, and interviews. In fact, I interviewed more than a hundred men and women regarding their own relationships and the lists they used to find their partners. They were single, divorced, newlyweds, and married people. Friends, friends of friends, and even strangers. Throughout the book, I will share poignant points of their stories. Stories are great, stories help us grow, and stories may remind us that some disheartening things are really just petty in the grand scheme of life.

Let's be honest—there are thousands of books on relationships. Instead of reading several books, you can read my notes and get a handle on the literature available. This is not supposed to be a purely academic book. It's supposed to be a thought-provoking yet concise guide.

There are no names to protect the privacy of my interviewees. But their stories will be so familiar to you that you will feel like you might know them—and you just might. But don't go around pointing the finger. You'll lose friends that way. Of course, I might lose friends too. Yikes.

Don't get me wrong; although I hate the saying that things happen for a reason, there is some truth to it. The reason why things happen may not be clear to us today. In fact, the reason might be as cloudy as a Starbucks London Fog, but in the long run, it all works out. Trust me.

Another thing that you should remember is that in life, there are no guarantees. No guarantees with love, with your career, with anything. And you really have only today.

As an old acting mentor would say . . . And here we are . . .

INTRODUCTION

It was the summer of 2010, and I felt lost. Okay, no, I wasn't lost. I was more depressed and angry. My boyfriend of more than eight years had broken up with me for a girl he met in Vegas. They got married less than a year later. We were supposed to get married. Well, at least I thought so.

I thought he was the one I was going to marry because he was perfect. He was my list.

One day, in a nursing school biology class, my friend and I were writing down characteristics of our potential mate. She wrote down a single characteristic (well, actually, it was a name): the UK singer Craig David. I wrote down fifty-five characteristics. Keep in mind, I was twenty-one, and idealism is my forte. Also, this list was not in any particular order. At least I hope it wasn't—I put "loves me" as number forty-five! Below is my old list annotated with my justifications ten years later.

1) Smart *(Really, this has to be a given; and yes, this could also mean street smarts.)*
2) Went to school/has training/certification
3) Witty, intellectual *(This could lead into the first point.)*
4) Funny *(Yes!)*
5) Goofy when appropriate
6) Ambitious *(Double yes!)*
7) Lifelong learner
8) Self-esteem/slight cockiness
9) Well-paying job
10) Hobbies that are not illegal *(I thought I needed to be specific!)*
11) Open-minded
12) Friendly, affectionate
13) Outgoing, social
14) Compassionate

15) Trustworthy
16) Understanding
17) Patient
18) Likes to listen and talk
19) Hard-working
20) Likes to be challenged
21) Loves spending time with me
22) Warm
23) Caring, kind, genuine
24) Considerate
25) Short hair
26) 5'11" to 6'3" *(I am 5'2" myself and wanted someone to give me shoe options.)*
27) No facial hair *(Admit it, ladies; razor burn is awful.)*
28) Lean/skinny and not smaller than me *(I think it's weird when the guy is smaller than the girl.)*
29) Good hygiene *(This should be a given.)*
30) Any ethnicity
31) Wears stylish clothes
32) Twenty-three to twenty-six, at most twenty-seven *(Remember, I was twenty-one at the time.)*
33) Nice clean, straight teeth and a good smile *(I love my dentist, and my orthodontist did great work on my teeth.)*
34) Long arms
35) Likes to hug/hold
36) Likes traveling

37) Drives a car
38) Has an older sister/younger sister *(Someone told me once that this is a must, because it means that the guy knows how to treat a lady. I think we need further studies on that idea.)*
39) Good relationship with family and friends
40) Respect *(Why was this number forty? I have no idea.)*
41) Owns one pair of dark-denim jeans *(I'm a big fan of denim myself, and the dark-denim thing is a personal preference—obviously. I think everyone looks better in darker rather than lighter denim.)*
42) Health/exercise *(It is so important to keep up with healthy habits!)*
43) Does not lie/is honest *(Again, this is way too late on the list.)*
44) Gives back to the people around him *(I am referring to volunteer work.)*
45) Loves me *(I seriously don't know why this is number forty-five!)*
46) No smoking or drugs
47) Social drinker
48) Forward and direct
49) Can have fun and knows how to relax *(Again, I don't know how this ended up so far down the list.)*

50) Does not have to like shopping/sports *(Funny! I think I really meant the opposite with regard to the shopping piece.)*
51) Encouraging, supportive
52) Charming
53) Creative/adventurous
54) Likes to try new things
55) Has good friends

I have to laugh a little when I reread this list. Some of the characteristics could be consolidated, and some could be let go of completely.

This list was golden. A few years later, I met my (now ex-) boyfriend. It was as if he personified my list. I distinctly remember telling my friends how perfectly he matched the list. Of course, I realize now, he personified a good majority of the list, but lacked a fair number of qualities that I now think are important.

Let me fast-forward through our relationship.

When we first met, I was working as a salesperson at the GAP. We were about to close the store, and I was in a hurry to usher people out. I mistakenly thought he was a customer, turned to look at him, and said, "Can I help you?" in an extremely snotty tone. In fact, it was his birthday, and he had just been hired as a sales associate. He responded with something like, "No, I'm a new hire," and all I could do was mumble an "Oh, that's nice," turn around, and think, *Oh my goodness. That is the hottest guy I have ever seen. I sure screwed that up!*

But I hadn't. And so it began.

Our first date was a walk around downtown after a shift at work. I was wearing a navy-blue hoodie with a white crew neck and jeans with a white canvas belt. I remember being excited and asking a coworker if my outfit was cute enough for the date. I had short hair and braces and often wondered why any guy would want anything to do with me. But he did, and our date first led to a short two-year relationship followed by another eight-year relationship. Yes, it was an on-again-off-again relationship. And then it ended. Almost as abruptly as it began. Of course I am excluding a lot of details: graduations, new homes, new careers, travels, and, of course, arguments.

I was sitting in a parking lot when he broke up with me over the phone. "She's the one," he said. "And when you find the one, you will know." I was crushed. I had thought he was the one, at least for me. Of course, that day ended with a lot of crying and a drunken fiasco that would rival any romantic comedy.

I wasn't going to go into details, but then again it might shed light on the dramatic hot mess that unfolded. After the conversation, I went to my local big-box bookstore, found a quiet area by the stationery, phoned up my high school friend, and cried. I ranted and raved and cried. I cried so much I thought that I was going to get kicked out. I didn't, thank goodness. But I did get some disapproving glances and shocked stares.

This was me: a twenty-nine-year-old girl, frustrated, defeated, alone.

Fast-forward to a liquor store. In the store, already rather tipsy (thanks to a stop at a friends house), I paused in front of a fridge full of sparkling wine. There was Cava in the adjacent fridge. I rested my head against the cool glass, reminiscing about our trip to Barcelona to the Freixenet winery. Soon I realized that I was blocking two youngish girls who were looking to get some coolers. I turned to them with a whiny and deflated "hi." I should have stopped but didn't stop there. "My boyfriend just dumped me and I'm so upset," I continued instead. The girls were bewildered, to put it mildly.

I ended the night at a high school friend's house, where four good friends saw a disheveled, upset Elena cry through a reenactment of our last phone call. I have to say it wasn't one of my brighter moments in life.

How did my list fail me? Did it change? Did he personify the list and then I changed? Did I really need a list?

A few months after the breakup, I had the opportunity to go on a spectacular girl getaway in Asia. My good friend and I discussed "the list," and she decided to make one of her own. A few months later, she met her boyfriend.

A few days before my thirtieth birthday, about one year after the breakup, I decided to switch up my list. This revised edition is in no ranking order either, but if you compare the two lists thus far, you will see that I've consolidated a few qualities.

1) Educated
2) Loves everything about me
3) Witty, funny, goofy when appropriate
4) Does not lie, can tell the truth, is honest and trustworthy
5) Can handle confrontation, is forward and direct *(I think that this point is the result of a learning process during the breakup.)*
6) Ambitious, will enrich my life, is encouraging and supportive
7) Has self-esteem but is not too cocky
8) Employed at a well-paying job
9) Has hobbies, reads
10) Friendly, affectionate, public displays of affection
11) Open-minded, thinks outside the box, is creative and adventurous, and likes to try new things
12) Outgoing and social
13) Compassionate/understanding/patient/thoughtful/respectful
14) Good communication

15) Warm/caring/genuine/considerate
16) Short hair
17) Taller than 5'9" *(I decreased my height restriction.)*
18) Lean *(not skinnier than me)*
19) Good hygiene
20) Loves to travel, has great relationships with friends and family
21) Has a sense of style
22) Thirty to thirty-six
23) Healthy, likes to exercise *(Again, I don't know why this is low on the list!)*

I decided that even though I had my heart broken by someone who fit the list, the list was something I would want to invest in again. Rather than succumb to Adele's "Someone Like You" or Amy Winehouse's "Back to Black," I decided that this time things were going to go differently.

The Ideal

Girls
are like apples
on trees. The best ones
are at the top of the tree.
The boys don't want to reach
for the good ones because they are afraid
of falling and getting hurt.
Instead, they just get the rotten apples
from the ground that aren't as good,

but easy. So the apples at the top think something is wrong with them, when in reality, they're amazing. They just have to wait for the right boy to come along, the one who's brave enough to climb all the way to the top of the tree.

- Anonymous

Why the List?

Let's talk about the basics. Sometimes writing stuff down helps. That's easy, right? It helps you focus. And really, it helps you reevaluate. Think of the difference between going to the grocery store with a list and without a list.

With a list, you might not stray away from your "must-haves." Sure, there might be a great sale on tomato soup or toothpaste, but generally, you are going to get things on your list *first*. When you have a list in front of you, you don't forget. When you have a list, the choices are clear and concise.

Without a list, you base your purchases on how hungry you are and end up grabbing random items you don't need, like pretzel-covered peanut-butter snacks. You might, in fact, wind up with duplicates. The reevaluation begins when you stare at your half-full grocery cart as you wait in line and realize that you don't really need half the stuff that you put in your cart. More often than not, you forget the one thing you went shopping for in the first place because it wasn't so apparent when you were browsing the shelves.

The List: Help or Hindrance?

Should a grocery list really be compared to a list of characteristics for a potential mate, someone you would like to spend the rest of your life with? I say yes.

One of my interviews was with a woman in her fifties who mentioned that the list should be used as a framework or guideline only, and that you should not get tied down to the list.

Here's another shopping analogy. In her book *Marry Him: The Case for Settling for Mr. Good Enough*, Lori Gottlieb talks about being either a satisfier or a maximizer. A satisfier goes to a clothing store looking for a sweater. She finds one she likes—the price, the fit, and the color. The satisfier buys the sweater and takes it home. The satisfier is . . . well, satisfied with the purchase. At the same time, the maximizer goes into the same store, sees the same sweater, and finds things wrong with it. The color isn't the exact shade she wants, the buttons are too distracting, and it's made of wool and she was really looking for a poly-cotton blend. The maximizer thinks the sweater is okay but also thinks that there must be something better. There might be a sale at the GAP, or Nordstrom might have the new fall collection already, or better yet, eBay might have something similar for less money. So the maximizer leaves the store and goes for the hunt, looking at several stores trying to find that perfect sweater. Alas, after some time, the maximizer comes back to the original store only to realize that the sweater is gone—the satisfier bought it.

Bottom line, don't be too picky or get caught up in too much detail. But what's the fine line?

According to J. M. Kearns's *Shopping for Mr. Right*, "Shop all the time, and when you see a good one, make your move . . . but a chance sighting of someone who could really be your life partner is so rare and so precious that it needs to be acted on" (Kearns 2011, 89). Good stuff.

Potato Soup versus Lobster Theory

Which one is more expensive—potato soup or lobster? Well, that's easy. The market-price lobster is more expensive. Which one is more rare? That's an easy question too. Which one is richer in flavor? The lobster keeps on winning! Of course, this analogy doesn't really apply to those who don't eat seafood.

But what if the lobster was a steak—a porterhouse sixteen-ounce steak? And I'm sure there are vegetarian options that are either high class or lowball.

How does this analogy pertain to dating and the list, you ask? Here's how: Why go through life with potato soup when you can have a lobster diet? Why do people settle for something mediocre if they could have a delicacy? Are people inherently lazy? Is a lobster too difficult to recognize? Or is the search for lobster so time consuming and frustrating that people tire of it and settle for something not quite so unique and rare?

Case in point. I knew someone who did just that. He was tired of being alone. Lucky for him an attractive girl came his way, and he was enamored. He forgot everything that he stood for—so for once he could feed his ego with someone whom he never thought would ever associate with him. His emotions and self-doubt took over, and all he could see were her 100-watt smile and her perfect skin. He fell for a superficial ideal and lost his soul. Truth be told, time will tell if his love for her will last through the ages, but for now it fills his own insecurity. It's a shame he has such insecurities (he's lovely!).

Or is it that people are insecure and don't think they are good enough and therefore attempt to mold themselves into an ideal that attracts the opposite gender? Don't get me wrong—I'm all for physical exercise and dressing in style, but

I realize that what really matters is an attitude adjustment: thinking positively and being comfortable in your skin. But it's hard to adjust your attitude when there are so many external factors. Can people suddenly switch their principles and live a happy life? For sure, as long as they make a full commitment to their new principles and shed all resentments from past values.

What about the matching hypothesis, which states that people of equal attractiveness are attracted to each other? It has more than an ounce of truth. We are served best in a relationship with people of equal attractiveness, because we are playing on a level field. If there is a discrepancy—if, for example, a good-looking man dates a moderately attractive gal—other factors such as money or status are involved. Think about some celebrity couples based on this matching hypothesis. Is it real love?

How Does the List Work?

Having a list is a starting point. Rhonda Byrne's best seller *The Secret* relates success and failure to that famous law of attraction. Drawing upon what you want the most, even if you have the list ready for action, you yourself must be in the right frame of mind. What does that mean? Barbara DeAngelis in *Are You the One for Me?* says it best: "If you aren't emotionally ready to be in an intimate relationship, you'll have a difficult time determining whether you're with the right person. The relationship won't feel right because of your own problems, not because you aren't compatible with your mate" (p. 364). So get your own life together *first*. Then start shopping. It will make it easier.

Questions to Ponder

1) What makes me happy?
2) Do I feel ready to be in a relationship? (Read: Have I dealt with the skeletons in my closet?)
3) Do I think that being in a relationship will make me complete?
4) What can I bring to a relationship?
5) When I am in a relationship, do I find myself constantly trying to change or improve the other person?

THE LIST

*Guys are like stars; there are a million of them,
but only one makes your dreams come true.*
—*Anonymous*

Development of the List

I didn't think that there was anything to the details of my list. I didn't have any baggage, and my experience was limited, so I was really left to my own devices when developing this list. Naturally, I referred to my own imagination, and *Grey's Anatomy*.

But there are other ways to create a list that works for you. Those of you who have a few relationships under your belt can use your experience to your advantage. Take the bad characteristics and add them to your "nay" column and add the good characteristics from the great people that you have met to the "yay" column.

Sometimes we don't know what we need until we're in a situation that isn't ideal. A whole learning process begins (hopefully). Note: the learning process is the hard part. Ever wonder why certain people seem to always date the same type of people? It's because they haven't learned from the previous situation.

Our lists of desired qualities change over time. They grow with us, shift with our situations, and adapt to current circumstances of our lives. As we grow and mature, so do our lists.

In her book *Are You the One for Me?* Barbara DeAngelis talks about six qualities everyone should look for in a partner. These qualities are general and apply to either gender. This list includes commitment to personal growth, emotional openness, integrity, maturity and responsibility, high self-esteem, and a positive attitude toward life.

Let's look at these characteristics further.

1) Commitment to personal growth: This means that the person is committed to learning how he or she can be better—at everything. It calls upon working together as a team and really trying to seek help when necessary. This becomes important when life throws you a curveball; you don't want a bailer.
2) Emotional openness: Bottom line, share your feelings. You're not a robot, so knowing that you have feelings and understand how to *appropriately* express them is important. Random emotional outbursts can be exhausting. Just saying.
3) Integrity: Don't lie; tell the truth, and be honest with yourself and with your partner. It sounds simple, but it's probably the hardest part of being in a relationship. Revealing who you really are to people whom you care about can be scary. And the truth hurts sometimes. Some people would rather lie to make a relationship continue smoothly than face the truth. I hate arguments myself – but sometimes they are necessary and crucial.
4) Maturity and responsibility: What does *mature* even mean? Mature people make enough money to support themselves and know how to take care of themselves and be responsible for their lives. A caveat of being responsible is being respectful. Maturity also means dealing with your problems like an adult. All the

tattle-telling and games are exhausting and a waste of time—your and your potential partner's time.
5) High self-esteem: "A person with low self-esteem loves in order to feel good about himself herself. A person with high self-esteem loves because he or she feels good about himself or herself" (p. 330). Enough said. Having self-esteem and willing to act on something often go hand in hand. Having the confidence to take risks is invigorating. A friend once told me, "Leap, and the invisible net will catch you."
6) Positive attitude toward life: Who really wants to be with a negative person? So much wasted energy. You create your own reality, and point of view is everything. I know there are difficult times and all you want to do is dwell on your sorrows. But turning that frown upside down is one step toward a happier reality.

DeAngelis identifies some important qualities. I think that most people show varying degrees of these characteristics, and the degree of these qualities that you need depends upon where you are in your life.

The Science behind the List

Believe it or not, there is science to support this idea of a list: evolutionary psychology. And thanks to the book, of the same title (Buss, 1999) I realized that it all goes back to reproduction, which is how life goes on. I mean, think about it: without babies, life as we know it would be at a standstill and we would eventually become the dinosaurs of our time—extinct.

Thankfully, we don't have that problem. And although families are not as large as they used to be, people are still reproducing.

First, let's look at women and the way they mate. I promise this won't be boring.

Women and Mating

I could compare women to some rare species of bird to illustrate that women's mating preferences have evolved, but since one of the major goals of evolution is ensuring that the species continues, you can imagine where this is going.

Women are selective. In short, they need to be selective because they need to make sure that their future children will survive and thrive and carry on. They need to make sure that their partner fits the bill; otherwise, women might be flying solo. Here comes the praise for all single parents out there: working, picking up the kids from school, and being two parents in one—you literally are modern-day superheroes!

Another reason why women are picky about their potential mate is that women face nine months of pregnancy fun. It involves gaining weight, moodiness, and perhaps even morning sickness and bed rest. This is not exactly appealing, although your hair gets shinier and you have that healthy glow. Men will have invested but a few minutes of their time to produce a child. Clearly, this is not the same level of commitment.

Now, here is where the list becomes a hindrance. Having a static list of characteristics might not take into account a prospective mate's future potential. Discounting a mate (or being too picky) based on the present only might leave you out in the cold. It's that whole shopping for a sweater thing with an evolutionary twist. Science—gets you every time!

All in all, women consult the list on a psychological level. Women are generally looking for mates who are willing to invest, who are able to physically protect themselves as well as their woman and child, who show good parenting skills, and who are compatible. Check out the chart.

Mating Characteristics	Evolved Mate Preference
Selecting a mate who is *able* to invest	Good financial prospect: Money or the ability to make money is attractive.
	Social status: High status tends to mean more resources and/or control of resources.
	Older age: Women tend to go for men who are three or more years older than they are. As status and wealth tend to rise with age, this becomes important.
	Ambition/industriousness: Men who work hard support the idea of higher social status and security.
	Size, strength, athletic ability: Physical ability is important.
Selecting a mate who is *willing* to invest	Dependability and stability: Being responsible, emotionally secure, and mature.
	Love and commitment cues: Showing the willingness to spend time, energy, and effort for the partner's benefit, even if it means tabling one's own needs.

Selecting a mate who is able to physically protect self, women, and children	Size (height) Strength Bravery Athletic ability: It all boils down to protection.
Selecting a mate who will show good parenting skills	Dependability Emotional stability Kindness Positive interactions with children
Selecting a mate who is compatible	Similar values Similar age Similar personality

If you check out the second list I made, you'll notice that much of it coincides with the chart of Mating Characteristics above.

Selecting a mate who is *able* to invest: is ambitious and educated, has self-esteem, is employed at a well-paying job

Selecting a mate who is *willing* to invest: loves everything about me, does not lie, can tell the truth, is honest and trustworthy, can handle confrontation, is forward and direct, has good communication skills, is warm/caring/genuine/considerate

Selecting a mate who is able to physically protect self, women, and children: is taller than 5'9", is lean (not skinnier than me), is healthy, and likes to exercise

Selecting a mate who will show good parenting skills: witty, funny, goofy when appropriate, friendly, affectionate, open-minded, compassionate, understanding, patient, thoughtful, and respectful

> **Selecting a mate who is compatible:** has hobbies, reads, has good hygiene, is thirty to thirty-six, loves to travel, has great relationships with friends and family, has a sense of style, thinks outside the box, is creative and adventurous, and likes to try new things

It looks like evolution has taught me well!

Now let's look at the results of my interview process. In my own poll, which included more than one hundred individuals, I asked women (single/married/divorced/partner) for the top three characteristics they were looking for in a potential mate, or, if they were married already, what they most appreciated in their mates.

Here are the top three characteristics:

1) Sense of humor and funny (tie)
2) Smart and honest (tie)
3) Kind

Sounds like the top three hit the key points of selecting a mate who is able and willing to invest and who will show good parenting skills.

When reviewing the results of the interviews, there were some characteristics that stood out. One wanted someone who was "able to build a house with their bare hands," which gives reference to selecting a mate who exhibits physical strength. Someone wanted a "missionary to lead them spiritually," which speaks to a mate who has similar values.

In one of my interviews, a woman stated that she didn't have a list for her potential mate; instead, she had a list for herself that described the person she wanted to become in the future. Her top three traits were:

1) Independent
2) Treating herself nicely
3) Having life and career goals

She worked hard to develop these characteristics. She would cook good meals for herself and buy herself flowers to treat herself nicely. She focused on her own career goals and how she could achieve them. As coincidence would have it, soon she met her husband at work.

Men and Mating

If women are looking for a mate for the long haul, where does that leave men? Commitment. Men who hold the promise of commitment may be able to attract a wider range of women. Being able to promise access to resources and a willingness to invest in children might also entice a potential mate. Commitment increases the odds of offspring and future generations.

But what are men looking for in a potential mate? There are similarities.

Mating Characteristics	Evolved Mate Preference
Selecting a mate who is able to reproduce	Youth/age: Men tend to go for women who are an average of two and a half years younger than they are. Physical appearance: Men tend to like full lips, clear/smooth skin, and good muscle tone and body fat distribution (small ratio of waist to hips). Behavior: A youthful gait, animated facial expression, and energetic appearance are attractive.
Selecting a mate who will show good parenting skills	Dependability Emotional stability Kindness Positive interactions with children
Selecting a mate who is compatible	Similar values Similar age Similar personality

Men look for a mate with a good reproductive status that comes with youthfulness as it shows in age, beauty, and behavior.

We all hear that biological clock ticking. It's true; it does tick. As women grow older, the ability to have children decreases. It may not tick as urgently as it did decades ago, as more women are having children into their late thirties or even early forties, but it sure does tick.

Physical appearance is important, and any cover girl on any magazine will tell you this means clear skin, nice hair, and white teeth. All those are a given, but the waist-to-hip ratio is fascinating. Studies reveal that the hourglass shape, a small waist with larger hips, is universally preferred.

Why is the hourglass shape a good thing? First, fat distribution around the waist is not good health-wise. It's often linked to diseases like diabetes and hypertension. That reason alone should have you working out your obliques. The waist-to-hip ratio reveals a long-term health status that also indicates reproductive status. While this by no means says that if you are not curvy you are not healthy, on a subconscious level, men pay attention to that. So, if you are single, the next time you go shopping, pay more attention to those curves and buy clothes that accentuate the small of your waist.

So, when I asked men about their top three characteristics in a potential mate, the following made the top three:

1) Attractiveness
2) Sense of humor
3) Intelligence/ambition

A recent online poll looked at the top ten traits that attract men to women.

YourTango teamed up with Glo.com and Chemistry.com and surveyed twenty thousand people to determine the answers to the burning question as to what attracts men to women. What did this poll find? Naturally, "sexual chemistry" and "smile" rank high when a man initially meets a woman, but as time marches on and fleshy excitement simmers, "kindness" and "sense of humor" ranked in the top spots.

Here's the official list of what *initially* attracts a man to a woman:

1. Sexual chemistry
2. Smile
3. Kindness
4. Sense of humor
5. General body type
6. Eyes
7. Intelligence
8. Communication skills
9. Teeth/lips
10. Hair

Five out of the ten traits deal with physical beauty. Surprising? Not really.

Here's what attracts a man to a woman in the *long term*:

1. Kindness
2. Sense of humor
3. Communication skills
4. Sexual prowess
5. Intelligence
6. Smile
7. Listening skills
8. Money/wealth
9. General body type/fitness
10. Eyes

When it comes to long-term commitment, however, men and women are on the same page.

The same online poll also asked women what they find most attractive in men at their first meeting:

1. Kindness
2. Sense of humor
3. Smile
4. Intelligence
5. Communication skills
6. Sexual chemistry
7. Listening skills

8. Eyes
9. Teeth/lips
10. Ambition

When it comes to long-term commitment, women look for the following:

1. Kindness
2. Sense of humor
3. Communication skills
4. Listening skills
5. Intelligence
6. Ambition
7. Smile
8. Sexual prowess
9. In a similar life stage as you
10. Location/close enough to see daily

The lists of initial and long-term traits women care about are almost identical.

List Gone Wrong

So you know what you want, your list is set, and you are in a good mental space. It should be easy to find a mate, right? Wrong. Two unfortunate issues can occur.

The first is slightly more annoying than the second. It falls under the category of deception. There are guys who are out to deceive women: the *douche bags*. We all know at least one, if not more. They are the ones who constantly send mixed signals and play games. That was cool when you were in college, but it is not so cool in terms of evolution. Jeff Mac's *Manslations: Decoding the Secret Language of Men* describes those men to a T.

Men who like the intensity of the beginning of a relationship—the butterflies, the flowers, the initial meetings—are the *romantics*. Then they get bored and they get out. On to the next.

Therapy addicts are the tortured souls who like to analyze everything and use self-help books to figure stuff out. They will help you "fix" things in your life.

For the *scorekeepers*, it's a numbers game and you are another notch on their belt. However they can get you in bed, they will try it. And then they will leave—maybe not the first time, but definitely the second. They want to have their cake and eat it too. STDs need not apply.

Having a lot of women interested at the same time is the goal of the *collectors*; they need to show that they've still got it—very similar to the goal of the scorekeepers.

"Honest" players say they aren't good for you, so you spend all the time trying to prove them wrong, because you are a good person and you want to believe people are inherently

good. So, when they eventually screw you over, they can't be blamed, because after all, they did warn you. For the record, I know these types all too well.

Now here is where ladies get stuck; we want to "fix" douche bags. But it's a waste of time. Move on. Some men may grow up (the ones who are actually smart), and some may not. Games are for juveniles, and the mature person who is right for you won't want to play lame games. Evolution has spoken: survival of the fittest! This is no exception.

I should know. I became involved in a quasi rebound. He was the total opposite of my ex. He was a professional who seemed to have it together. I was gravely mistaken, as I found myself wrapped up in his smooth-talking ways and in love with his potential. I couldn't see that it was not a great fit, because I didn't realize that I was trying to fill the gap of my previous relationship. It wasn't about him; it was all about me. It took awhile, but with the help of a friend I was finally able to see that. I should have gotten my act together before embarking on another relationship. I'm sorry he got disheveled with my feelings, and I wish him all the best.

The second issue that arises is having to weigh the importance of the attributes you are seeking in a mate. Not all men are created equal. Sure, the mate might not embody the full list, but what characteristics on the list are deal breakers for you? So he doesn't own a pair of dark-denim jeans and he doesn't seem to designate one side of the sink for dirty and the other for clean dishes. Does it matter?

I was meeting my friend's new guy for the first time, and she wanted me to pay special attention to two things: his height and his demeanor. Obviously, she was attracted to tall guys; after all, her ex was six feet, but this new guy was not. She was worried about that. She was also attracted to a certain friendliness her ex-boyfriend exhibited. He could walk in a room of strangers and make small talk with anyone. He was very outgoing, funny, and personable.

At a small gathering, I finally met him, and we talked about building his practice and his family. It was a conversation of quality over quantity. To be honest, I did not even notice that the guy was eye level to my friend. What I did notice instead was his demeanor. He was very genuine. Rather than being outgoing and friendly, he was quiet and reserved. He worked steadily, preparing the food in the kitchen to keep the flow of the party going.

Two things to note:

1) Opposites attract: My friend's case was extreme, which often happens after breakups. It happened to me for sure. You're dating a certain type of person, and if it does not work, you gravitate toward the exact opposite. More often than not, the person right for you is somewhere in the middle.

2) Weighing someone's benefits: This really goes back to analyzing your list and pinpointing your values. Should physical characteristics really pull most of the weight? After all, what you look like today will not guarantee what you look like thirty years from now. And, in my opinion, an ugly personality overshadows a pretty face any day.

Questions to Ponder

1) What would be on your list?
2) What are your deal breakers?
3) How are you valuing certain characteristics on your list?
4) Are you allowing outside influences (family, friends) to dictate what is on your list?
5) If you are currently in a relationship, does your partner fit your list?

Waiting: The Crazy Cat Lady Lingers

*My knight in shining armor turned out
to be a loser in aluminum foil.*
—*Anonymous*

Breakups are hard. No one said they would be easy. I think as people get older, there is that lingering thought that the pickier they are, the more likely they are to end up alone. So here is my ode to the research book that drove me crazy, Lori Gottlieb's *Marry Him: The Case for Settling for Mr. Good*

Enough. The book hurt. No happy ending, no rainbow or sunshine. It's the straight goods. Don't be so picky, because otherwise you will end up alone. Maybe those friends who were just friends—those you never considered romantically at all—should perhaps be looked at again. Maybe what you have now isn't going to get any better, so be thankful and suck it up, buttercup.

You can tell why *Marry Him* enraged me and sent me on a tirade of fear and self-loathing. I didn't think I could possibly become the crazy cat lady. I mean, I have style, I work out, and I'm social. There is no way that could happen. Yet I would see young, happy couples on the sidewalk and just want to push them into traffic. Of course, I never wanted anyone to get hurt, and never would have acted on these feelings, but misery definitely loves company. Why did they have happy relationships and I didn't? It wasn't fair. Life isn't fair, sunshine.

My mind began to swell with a million bad thoughts. What if I was not charming enough for a guy to want to be with me? What if *Manslations* was right? Maybe that first impression was crucial.

Two of my girlfriends share the same "predicament." Both are in long-term relationships. Both purchased property with their mate and cohabitate. Both women are not married but are convinced that a ring is just around the corner. What was hold up? (P.S. Both are happily married now). For a girl who wanted to put off getting married until she had her own TV show, it was surprising that I found myself wishing I were nesting with someone. My coworker and I attended a party at Tiffany's, and I tried on the six-carat ring that was priced at half a million dollars. It felt like nothing. It felt like nothing because it wasn't from anyone special. It meant nothing except for the fact that something that cost as much as a house was resting on my finger.

It's hard to accept that even fashion seems to say that it is normal and therefore best to be in a relationship. It doesn't help that the "boyfriend look" is in right now. You know, the baggy jeans that could have been your boyfriend's, or the oversized cardigan, except it's slightly fitted and you paired it with cute ballet flats a la Katie Holmes. Just embrace it; trends will come and go.

Okay, I am ranting. But when you are single and you have a list, waiting for the list to come to fruition is agonizing. And then the crazy starts. You act out in ways that you never thought you would. I'm going to spare you the details of my personal version of crazy, but crazy happens to everyone somehow, somewhere.

The 2009 movie *Up in the Air*, starring George Clooney, Vera Farmiga, and Anna Kendrick, is a great movie about relationships. In a scene from the movie, Natalie (Anna Kendrick) talks to Alex (Vera Farmiga) and Ryan (George Clooney) about her recent breakup with her boyfriend.

NATALIE

When I was sixteen, I thought by twenty-three I would be married, maybe have a kid . . . corner office by day, entertaining at night. I was supposed to be driving a Grand Cherokee by now.

ALEX

Life can underwhelm you that way.

NATALIE

Now I have my sights on twenty-nine, because thirty is just way too . . . apocalyptic. I mean, where did you think you'd be by . . . *(Natalie catches herself, having no idea how old Alex is.)*

ALEX

It doesn't work that way.

RYAN

At a certain point, you stop with the deadlines.

ALEX

They can be a little counterproductive.

NATALIE

I don't want to say anything that's . . . antifeminist. I mean, I really appreciate everything your generation did for me.

ALEX

(My generation?) It was our pleasure.

RYAN

Well done.

NATALIE

But sometimes it feels like no matter how much success I have, it all won't matter until I find the right guy.

ALEX

You really thought this guy was the one.

NATALIE

Yeah, I guess. I don't know. I could have made it work. He just really fit the bill.

RYAN

The bill?

NATALIE

My type. You know, white collar. College grad. Loves dogs. Likes funny movies. Six foot one. Brown hair. Kind eyes. Works in finance but is outdoorsy, you know, on the weekends. *(We think she's done.)* I always imagined he'd have a single-syllable name like Matt or John or . . . Dave. In a perfect world, he drives a Four Runner, and the only thing he loves more than me is his golden Lab. Oh . . . and a nice smile. *(Back to Alex and Ryan)* How about you? *(This catches both Alex and Ryan off guard.)*

RYAN

I'm not sure if . . .

NATALIE

I meant Alex . . .

RYAN

Right.

ALEX

Huh, let me think for a sec. *(Mulls it over)* Well, by the time you're thirty-four, all the physical requirements are pretty much out the window. I mean, you secretly pray he'll be taller than you. *(Ryan smiles.)* Not an asshole would be nice. Just someone who enjoys my company, comes from a good family. You don't think about that when you're younger. *(Thinking)* Wants kids . . . Likes kids . . . Wants kids. Healthy enough to play catch with his future son one day. *(We can tell Ryan is taking a serious interest in this.)* Please let him earn more than I do. That doesn't make sense now, but believe me, it will one day. Otherwise, it's just a recipe for disaster. *(Reaching)* Hopefully some hair on his head . . . ? But it's not exactly a deal breaker anymore. Nice smile . . . Yep, a nice smile just might do it. *(Alex looks to Ryan. He has a nice smile.)*

NATALIE

Wow. That was depressing. *(Alex and Ryan react. It's not that bad.)*

How do you get out of the crazy funk? Well, for starters, get off the couch and move. Do something good—like really karmically good. And while I know it's easy to say and hard to do, I will say it: Stop dwelling on what you don't have and look at what you do have. Turn that frown upside down. Change comes from within, and when it's time, you just have to do it. You'll know what you have to do if you trust yourself.

Two things to remember in dealing with a broken heart:

1) Embrace the crazy: Only truly crazy people say they are not crazy. As you get through the mundane every day and something gets you discombobulated, just remember to embrace it. Times are tough, and whatever won't kill you will only make you stronger. Maybe try not to text people whose potential you are in love with when you're drunk. It may make for a great story when you are older—much older. What makes an even better story is if the person you texted when you were drunk actually responds. While in a romantic comedy this might happen, it's not that likely in real life. In real life, your text will just confirm the person's hunch that you are crazy and give iPhone evidence to prove it.

Let me clarify: by "embracing the crazy" I don't mean doing something that would hurt you or others, damage property, or do anything else that's illegal. Don't make matters worse. But don't take yourself too seriously when you slip up and commit TWI (texting while intoxicated) or when you find yourself reminiscing about past vacations at the sight of a Cava bottle.

As an inquiry, I sent the following text to three guys I knew:

Here is a business proposition for you. It's entitled the Backup Contract. It starts whenever the two parties sign the agreement, and it will last for two and a half years. At the end of two and a half years, if both parties are single (and unattached), several options are available: The two people either get married or the two people walk away from the agreement and the contract is void. Should there be a disagreement, such as one person wants to get married and the other one does not, then the person who wants to walk away pays the other person $1,000. Thoughts?

I received two rejections and one refused to answer. A year later, I sent the exact same text out and got all rejections. The point is to set a time limit of one year or less to crazy propositions you make to your friends when you are getting over a breakup. Have fun and ask away.

Which leads to the next point:

2) You are better than this: Whatever your version of crazy was, it's a phase. You aren't really like that. We know. Don't explain it. Just keep calm and carry on. Go to therapy. Don't be ashamed if you need a therapist; it's always good to talk to someone who is impartial. This is the perfect makeover time.

Hit the gym, go back to school, and write a book. Hey, wait a minute—this sounds like someone I know!

One day, I went for a walk and passed a church. Couples were scattered on the lawn, in the parking lot, and across the street. It seemed as if they had a task. Ah yes, marriage prep. As I continued on my walk, I saw an old lady carrying a bag of cat food. Coincidence? I think not. She might just love cats and have a loving husband at home. Maybe not.

After reading Lori Gottlieb's *Marry Him: The Case for Settling for Mr. Good Enough*, I was slightly depressed. Yes, the book totally challenged my views on how easy it would be to find someone compatible. So I turned to the same place where I found *Marry Him* and found Christine Whelan's book *Marry Smart*.

Marry Smart saved my book from becoming a crazy monologue about a newly single girl. The author of *Marry Smart* talks about SWANS—"Smart Women Achievers No Spouse." I thought it was catchy. The book details how SWANS are the way of the future. It really starts with choice. Everyone has choices, whether to get married and have two kids by twenty-eight, or travel and finish school when you are thirty-four. Choices are everywhere, and you shouldn't feel bad for wanting more, wanting less, or wanting something different. It's your decision. Now, there will always be those seemingly jealous people who think that just because you have ambition, dreams, and desires for your own life, you are putting other things aside (like starting a family and settling down). Nowadays, it isn't like that at all. I'm a firm believer in doing everything at once and doing it well. *Marry Smart* confirmed that my go-getter attitude isn't a bad thing at all. It sets me apart, and like the crazy, I should embrace it.

Questions to Ponder

1) My old acting mentor used to tell me to take account of my positive inventory. What sets you apart from others and makes you unique?
2) Have you sacrificed your dreams for the happiness of others?
3) What are your goals for the year? The next five years? The next ten years?
4) Are you living the life you want to lead?
5) What is your biggest fear in life?

Master's Degree in Love

Normal is only a cycle on the washing machine.
—Anonymous

I decided to go back to school and ended up meeting some great colleagues who will definitely make an impact on the business world. I was the youngest and only single gal in the class. But going through the six-month boot camp portion of the program has led me to some unique observations. I mean, it doesn't always have to be about business, right?

Operations—The Process

I managed to share my sob story with one of my classmates, and as we were learning about operational flow maps, he decided that I needed such a flow chart to work out my dating kinks. See the following chart. All jokes aside, I do believe that this is an accurate assessment of dating at the very core.

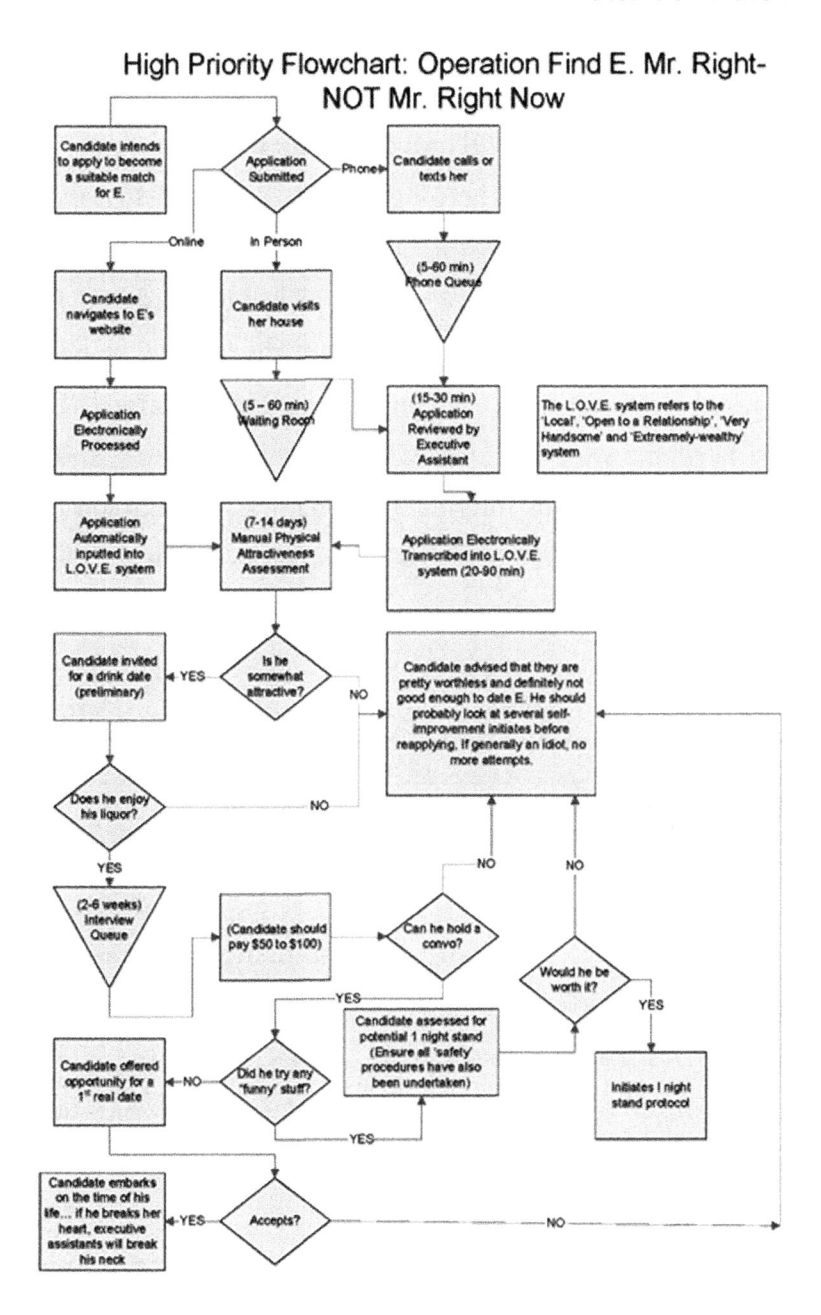

High Priority Flowchart: Operation Find E. Mr. Right - NOT Mr. Right Now

- Candidate intends to apply to become a suitable match for E.
- Application Submitted
  - Online → Candidate navigates to E's website → Application Electronically Processed → Application Automatically inputted into L.O.V.E. system
  - In Person → Candidate visits her house → (5–60 min) Waiting Room
  - Phone → Candidate calls or texts her → (5-60 min) Phone Queue → (15-30 min) Application Reviewed by Executive Assistant → Application Electronically Transcribed into L.O.V.E. system (20-90 min)

The L.O.V.E. system refers to the 'Local', 'Open to a Relationship', 'Very Handsome' and 'Extreamely-wealthy' system

- (7-14 days) Manual Physical Attractiveness Assessment
- Is he somewhat attractive?
  - YES → Candidate invited for a drink date (preliminary) → Does he enjoy his liquor?
    - YES → (2-6 weeks) Interview Queue → (Candidate should pay $50 to $100) → Did he try any 'funny' stuff?
      - NO → Candidate offered opportunity for a 1st real date → Candidate embarks on the time of his life... if he breaks her heart, executive assistants will break his neck
      - YES → Candidate assessed for potential 1 night stand (Ensure all 'safety' procedures have also been undertaken) → Accepts?
        - YES → (loops back)
        - NO → (exits)
    - NO → Can he hold a convo?
      - YES → (to 1 night stand assessment)
      - NO → Would he be worth it?
        - YES → Initiates 1 night stand protocol
        - NO → Candidate advised that they are pretty worthless and definitely not good enough to date E. He should probably look at several self-improvement initiates before reapplying. If generally an idiot, no more attempts.
  - NO → Candidate advised that they are pretty worthless and definitely not good enough to date E...

43

Strategy, or What's Your Game Plan?

My strategy professor will probably want to hide under a rug if he ever reads this, but here it goes. One day in class we were discussing a product-customer matrix. One student piped up, saying that this was how she had picked her husband. Of course, I needed to know more. So on the last day of class, I asked her what her comment meant. She explained that she needed a way to choose who was right for her without having her emotions interfere. She made a pro-and-con list with weighted criteria, otherwise known as a matrix. Here is a simple matrix example.

	Bryan	Kyle	Jason	Matt
Has a job	X	X		X
Wants a family		X	X	
Great personality		X	X	X

Please note: These are random names and random characteristics for the purpose of an example only. It would seem that Kyle is the lucky guy.

I realized that when I was ready to date, I needed a whole strategy behind it. Dating in your thirties is much different from dating in your twenties.

First of all, a lot of people are married or engaged to be married when they have reached their thirties, and there are fewer single friends. It's harder to break into new circles if you don't have an in, and even new circles don't guarantee a crowd of singles. In fact, moving to another city, for example, doesn't even guarantee a better selection of singles. As I said before, nothing is guaranteed.

By your thirties, many people have already been in more than one long relationship. If you haven't, you are rare and remain untainted by all the mistakes past relationships could entail. By your thirties people come with a whole lot of baggage and are (usually) playing for keeps. They aren't willing to play the games that someone in his or her midtwenties would play and are no longer inclined to put up with people's qualms. Usually people are more methodical and have a direct focus on the future. Then again, there are also those who would rather not be "tied" down, because their singlehood is too important to them, giving them the freedom that some married people yearn for. There are also those who are just starting their careers and need to catch up with their stagnant social lives. (The grass is always greener on the other side.)

That aside, some things change, but the feelings of euphoria don't. You can feel smitten at any age, and the feeling of your heart skipping a beat feels the same whether you are sixteen or sixty.

Elena Murzello

Diversifying Your Portfolio

Upon the suggestion from people in my life, I decided to join a dating website. Yup, I did it, and I only told five people that I did. Others might have figured it out, but I mainly kept the whole idea of online dating to myself. I believe I told people I was meeting people through friends of friends.

Online dating can be like *The Bachelorette*: If you're lucky, you'll have many prospects wanting to get to know you. They each will have a unique personality. I opened my matches up to all of North America. I had heard that the norm of online dating was, although one person could be talking to you, they could also be talking to ten different people at the same time.

I was looking for numbers at this point, so I decided to be ballsy and contact potential suitors. There were quite a few.

I soon I found myself e-mailing a bunch of guys who I thought might work out, though they all missed a certain something. I couldn't determine whether I was contacting them because I thought there could be a potential relationship or because I needed the practice.

Well, I did need the practice—practice talking with guys and practice remembering that excited feeling I would get when I saw a particular name pop up on my cell or received an e-mail from that person. It made me happy. It made me smile.

What did I learn from the online dating experience?

1) If you don't take things personally, time won't be wasted. We live in a world where information exchange/transfer is instantaneous, which means that the getting-to-know-you process can be expedited by e-mail and text. You may spend time getting to know someone who doesn't want to actually meet you. Don't take it personally. This also goes for people you meet in person but stop communicating with after the first or second date. Nothing is wrong with you, and the faster you move on and recognize that, the better. It's definitely a hard lesson to learn, but in the end, it's worth it.

    Dates can seem like nonspeaking commercial auditions. Let me explain. When you go into a nonspeaking commercial audition, more often than not it is your winning personality that will grant you the callback (a.k.a. the second date). Knowing your name is just the start; it's really knowing your own competitive advantage that will see you through. First dates are difficult because you are nervous and anxious. Knowing how to relax and let your personality shine is key. Doing this without alcohol in your system is crucial. Show your true colors.

2) Stick to your list. This can be easier on some online dating sites than others. Answering a long

questionnaire can help you weed out what you are not looking for. Of course, a computerized system can't fully know what you are looking for; some personal weeding-out will be necessary as well.
3) Give people a chance—a real chance. Meet them, and not just begrudgingly. My old high school principal used to say, "Respect begets respect." It's true. Give people the chance to show you who they are.
4) Be confident in who you are, and have respect for yourself. Know that you are enough and someone will like you today for who you are at this moment—not who you will become or who you once were. Another friend told me this: "A lady waits for no man." So don't wait around if he's not interested. Don't be the friend thinking the status will eventually wear him down. Have some self-respect; don't ask why, and instead just carry on with business as usual.

Example A: The Layered Relationship (a.k.a. the Rebound)

Everyone has heard of the rebound. The rebound is the person you hang out with, date, or sleep with after you break up with someone or after someone breaks up with you. In theory, it's a great idea to rebound with someone. Isn't meeting someone new the best way to get over someone? Not always.

In fact, people who need to find someone else to build up their "courage" actually reveal that they can't really be alone. As much as they would like to step up and be the man or independent women, the thought of being alone leaves them shell-shocked.

They jump into a relationship where they are told what to do all of the time. This relationship works until the people involved start resenting each other. The dominant one can't respect someone who always bends to his or her needs. And the not-so-dominant person can't get a word in edgewise. The relationship is doomed.

Or they jump into a relationship where they are in control because the partner is a lost soul, someone who needs guidance, or someone who needs to be taken care of. And the person who needs guidance will adore the person in control for mending a bruised ego. Will being the needed one be better than being the wanted one? Perhaps. Time will tell.

Of course there are relationships that have a little of both, where the give-and-take creates a more equal relationship. These relationships are few and far between, and many of these people will end up celebrating a seventy-fifth wedding anniversary among generations of friends and family.

Example B: String versus Ribbon

People say that they don't want to be strung along and they don't want to be second string. You're smart. Being the string sucks. Sure, string is dependable; it's the tie that binds, but string is often the neglected one. It's neglected compared to the ribbon.

Ribbon is rich, shiny, and dynamic. Think of the white satin ribbon that adorns a Tiffany's box. That ribbon makes the box special.

Here are the rules: Everyone is someone's ribbon. Everyone should be treated like ribbon. Stringing people along is neither respectful nor fair; it's rude.

I once had to tell a guy that I did not want to go out with him again right after the first date. I didn't want to waste my time or his. I felt horrible, as there was nothing wrong with him, except he was not the right person for me. Though it seems heartless and premature, sometimes you just know that it's not right, and no matter how many times you go out, the situation won't change.

In these cases, it's best to cut the tie swiftly, like a Band-Aid—the sooner the better. No time lost. No residual feelings spared.

There is a fine line between bending over backward, changing your behavior to suit another's demands or requirements, and compromise. Compromise is a mutual symbiosis, whereas the bending is one-sided.

The best date from the online was a guy named Jason. He was smart, nice, and charming. We checked out the local Dale Chihuly museum in Seattle, one summer afternoon.

Then we wandered around town, walking and talking and getting to know each other. It became apparent that we were very similar—almost too similar regarding the fact that we were both incredibly busy. We were both in school and working full time.

E-mails dwindled; I wanted him to let me know how to proceed. Please note, I wasn't asking him to marry me but merely to let me know if he wanted me to be more than a friend—if he wanted to take a chance on me, knowing that our busy schedules might keep us apart for most of the year.

Most logical people would say no, right? He was logical and did so: he said no.

Months passed, and I decided to e-mail him again. I don't know why, but he didn't respond until three months later. He talked about his travels and school and the weather. He wanted to know what I was up to. It was a nice, friendly e-mail, but it was an e-mail you would send to a long-lost pen pal. There was nothing personal about it, nothing that showed particular interest in me.

I deleted his message. Granted, we were never dating, and he didn't owe me anything, but I felt as if I was being treated like a string—a pen pal for when things got monotonous. Maybe this was his way of testing the waters—but come on. It was a new year, and it was too little too late. I was definitely not looking for a pen pal, so I felt justified in dropping him.

Reallocation of Resources

For the record, I did meet some interesting guys online.

Brent: A lawyer. Smart, but with attitude. He was good-looking, ran, played volleyball, and really enjoyed his P90x. He claimed his parents' forty-year relationship was an inspiration to him. Most of our chats involved him discussing his workouts, which I found slightly interesting. He had a large ego, which made him amusing.

Dave: A kind, witty, family-orientated business guy who liked girls who were ambitious but didn't want to be tied down. Although he said that he was communicating with only me, I found that hard to believe given our texts and phone calls were rare. We had set a date to meet the day after school ended for the summer, but much to my dismay, he texted and said he didn't think we would "click."

Adam: An older, bald professor of communications who had been overseas and had come back only to realize that all his friends were married and had moved on. He met me at a restaurant on possibly the hottest day (weather-wise) of the year. Sitting outside on the sweltering patio, I had had to excuse myself to blot the sweat off my forehead because I had rushed to the restaurant. When we moved into the restaurant, I was more interested in the curtains than the conversation. He talked about his travels and getting his

PhD. Two drinks in, I used my parents' anniversary (true) as my exit strategy.

Tim: An older divorced doctor from the suburbs looking for someone to spend his life with. Halfway through dinner, I wanted to leave. It was too noisy for him, the Japanese food was not what he had expected, and it was cold outside. I think his Syrian accent made it hard for us to understand each other, which annoyed me. Toward the end of the night, he said that he was proud of me, for working out, going to school, and writing a book. Proud of me? He didn't even know me!

Ed: A tall, outdoorsy guy from the UK who had just arrived in the country. He was the only guy I ended up going out with on two dates, but I think it only turned out that way because I had been somewhat aggressive about setting a follow-up. The first date, I managed to get blisters on my feet from walking around the city in my flip-flops. I began to realize through our conversation that Ed had come to the city to change his life. He wanted to try his hand in the movie industry and leave his stable career behind. At dinner, our conversation seemed to have more flow; I felt as if we could have chatted on a bus and it wouldn't have mattered. He made no compliments or any gestures that suggested that he actually liked me. My friend asked me afterward if he had complimented me at all. I realized that he had said absolutely nothing kind or considerate about me.

The serial dating was hard, and I only lasted on the website for the free three-month trial. I became very frustrated with the process and felt like I was not only wasting my time, but also the time of others as well. Did any of the guys that I met fit my bill? Sure. But the lack of chemistry was apparent enough to put a halt to further communication.

My favorite question I asked during my interviews was for people to share with me their worst and best date. Here are the results.

Worst Date:

> "It was an online date. The guy looked nothing like his picture. He was late, and I ended up getting a parking ticket!"

> "The car broke down, and we spent the whole evening waiting for it to be fixed."

> "I was left alone while camping, because he wanted to play Ultimate Frisbee. The next day he came back for me." (Please note that this woman married this man.)

> "The highlight of the evening was when I walked into a glass door and cut my nose."

"An accountant. We met online. He didn't talk to me during dinner and insisted we go Dutch on the bill."

"The guy kept talking about his 'old lady' and how he wished she would move out. I asked him why he was on a dating site, and he said he was just preparing for the future."

"Over dinner he told me he only dates Asian girls. He also mentioned that he heard all Filipino girls are crazy. And then we went Dutch."

"A blind date. Unfortunately, I agreed to meet at my place (he was supposed to just pick me up). He showed up with a bottle of wine, suggesting to have a glass before we go out. While having that glass of wine, he realized I had short hair and stated, 'I don't like short hair, but if you grow it out, we can continue.' I really don't need to tell the rest. I kicked him out before the bottle of wine was even half-done."

"I invited a girl to lunch, and she invited a mutual friend to come with us."

This is probably the worst dating story I have heard:

"I went on two dates with a girl. The first date, we had agreed to meet for dinner at a restaurant and, if it went well, go to a movie afterward. I ended up waiting at the restaurant for an hour and a half before she showed up (talk about embarrassing). The waitresses kept coming and asking if I wanted to order or if I was still hoping she would show up. When she finally did show up, she proceeded to drink a *lot* of wine and get pretty smashed.

I could tell she was really nervous about the date, but she still drank way too much. After dinner, she asked if I could drive her to my place so she could sober up before going home. My place was about ten minutes away, and hers was about forty-five minutes. Not wanting to make this girl drive home drunk, I drove her to my place and got her some coffee. At this point I am completely not into this girl anymore, and I'm starting to wish I had just left the restaurant and not waited for her to show up. She ends up throwing up a few times in the bathroom, then passing out in my bed, and despite my best efforts, she would not wake up. So I went to my computer and worked while I waited for this girl to sober up and get out of my house. Fast-forward to 5:00 a.m. She finally is sober enough to drive home, and I kick her out.

"About a week later, this girl calls me up and apologizes and wants to make it up to me and invites me out for a second date. For some reason, I agree and drive out to her place to pick her up. (OMG, what was I thinking?) I get to her house, and she answers the door in a panic and explains to me she forgot she had a huge presentation/project due for her architectural school the next day. I say it's no problem and suggest we go out another day, but she begs me to help her finish her project. She knows I have decent Photoshop and 3-D modeling skills and realizes I could help her create her presentation boards and enhance her renderings of buildings. So I agreed to help her a bit, thinking it will probably only take a few hours and could be kind of fun. (Seriously, what was I thinking?) I end up trying to leave around 11:00 p.m., but she begs me to stay until the project is done and starts crying/freaking out . . . At this point, every piece of me is saying to run the hell out the door and change my phone number, but for some reason I decide to help her out. I ended up staying up till 10:00 a.m. the next morning doing her project for her while she sobbed in her bedroom! She thanks me profusely, and we leave her place at the same time, her to go present her project and me to go home and sleep. I asked her not to call me again. I did later find out she got an A– on the project! I felt pretty proud of myself. Ha-ha."

Best Date:
There is definitely a trend—the best dates seem to be simple. No big-budget productions—it's the company that really makes the date memorable and fun.

"Had a coffee date that turned into a picnic."

"Met through mutual friends at a concert, and there was something unique."

"Spent all day hanging out, had brunch, went kayaking."

"Drove to Portland and ate Subway."

"Movie and cheap dinner. Laughed a lot and talked in the car."

"Sushi and a moonlit walk at the bay."

"We spent the entire day walking around the city and talking. I felt as though I had known him forever. He asked me if I would like to continue the date with dinner, and I agreed."

"My best date was a simple walk. I can't sit still when I'm nervous, so walking puts my energy to good use, and I get some exercise at the same time."

Return on Investment (ROI)

Sometimes even when people match each other's list, timing and distance could be an issue. But it's worth trying a relationship with logistical problems, because you really only live once. And life isn't about playing it safe; it's about taking the risks and reaping the benefits when things work out. Sometimes things might not work out, but it's a lesson learned and another story you can tell your girlfriends over cocktails.

It's a lot like an audition—putting everything out there to book the job—only this time, you're playing yourself in the story of your life. Auditioning over and over again and putting yourself through that roller-coaster ride is difficult and frustrating. But we do it because one day we will book that huge job and it will make all the awkward moments seem like simple blessings in disguise.

One day the person who fits the role perfectly will come along.

Questions to Ponder

1) What is my dating strategy—date the masses versus selective dates?
2) Am I a hardy individual? Am I able to cope with stress easily?
3) Is there a pattern to the people I am attracted to? Are they similar somehow?
4) When I go on a first date, do I try to relax and be in the moment?
5) What was your best and worst date? Why?

Interview Notes

I started this book thinking about lists and other people's lists.

Soon I decided that I needed to interview people. It was easy enough to come up with questions.

Some were relevant. Some were not.

I set up interviews with people—tons of people—some whom I had never met.

Depending on whether the people were married or single, attached or divorced, I gave them different sets of questions.

As I interviewed more and more people, I found that my interest shifted from my questions to people's stories.

And I got stories.

The most fascinating thing was that people were willing to open their hearts and tell me things in confidence.

Here are some of the responses that provoked my thoughts.

In my interviews with married folks, I asked the following:

> *Question: Upon your first meeting, did you know that you were going to marry?*

In *How Not to Marry the Wrong Guy,* Ann Milford and Jennifer Gauvain talk about a guy who knows that a girl is right for him within the first few meetings because there is a visceral feeling surrounding the event. Of course, the married women I interviewed talked about this as well.

"There was a sort of a spark."

"Possibly. I was attracted to him, and he was better quality than previous boyfriends."

"I knew I would be in his life. Not as far as getting married."

"There was a definite pull, and it kept us going back over nine years."

"I just fell in love, immediately knew. I can't explain."

The married men also had similar comments.

"Not the first but the second date."

"Early in the relationship, there were feelings."

"After our third date, I knew that marriage was a strong possibility."

"I didn't know at the beginning of the date, but I definitely knew before my date was over. We'd gone for drinks at a couple different places and then went back to my apartment to meet my two roommates that she also knew from high school. As the two of us were walking up the stairs to my apartment, I knew at that moment that I wanted to marry her."

Those answers almost make me barf. I mean, what is that? Obviously, I have never felt that immediate attraction to someone, or I would be trying to describe it right now. But maybe it's the mixture of butterflies when something exciting is going on and a euphoria that makes an internal soundtrack go off in your head. I have definitely felt that before. Man, if I packaged it up and put it in a bottle, I would be loaded. Or has it been done and called vodka?

I asked this question because I needed to know if I was missing something. How common was it that people just knew? I was pleased to find out that it was not as common as the literature suggests. A lot of people thought I was being crazy. More often than not, people suggested that their current mate had to grow on them, kind of like fungus, before they started to see him or her as a potential mate.

A word on the whole love-at-first-sight thing: As sappy as it is, it might be quasi-true. There might not be music playing in your head, but first impressions are important. According to J. M. Kearns's *Shopping for Mr. Right*, "you can detect a whole lot about someone when you first set eyes on them: not just whether you find them attractive, but also whether you like their style and their attitude, whether they have a corporate vibe or seem of freer stock. And whether they are interested in you" (Kearns 2011, 89).

Question: How did you meet?

There are some great stories on how people meet their mates. Some are straight out of romantic movie scripts, in which the couple's lives intertwined for years until they finally were together. People have met their matches online, through mutual friends, at work, or because of common interests. Similarly, when asked where single people try to meet their potential mates, people say friends, work, and common interests are a few ways through which to find a match. As with anything else, some people are positive and some are negative. Some singles I interviewed thought that they had exhausted all their options and were destined to be alone forever. Some are a little bit bitter, and in talking to them and listening to their stories, I can see why. I almost wanted to reach out and give these people a hug and tell them that what they were feeling is pain. Pain comes in different shapes and sizes, and the saying that "whatever doesn't kill you makes you stronger" is true. I wanted to tell them to take this as an opportunity to rise above. I may not have told them this, so I am telling this to you now.

Question: Do you believe in the "the one"?

Talk about "the one" is bittersweet. I got three answers to this question in my interviews: yes, no, and maybe. Why did I even bother with this question? Perhaps "the one" and lists are connected. Your significant other might transcend your list and become your "one" in reality. Am I getting too philosophical here?

Yes, I believe in "the one."

"Yes, but it's not for everyone."

"Whoever you decide when you are
ready, then that is the one."

"I don't think there are very many people out there that I can be truly happy with over the long term."

"I do, and I think everyone has a soul mate. However, one has to look for the person so you can't just sit back for the person to find you."

"It depends; if your partner can change and adapt at the same pace, then they are truly the one."

"Yes, I've always believed in a force that we cannot explain or understand: fate."

"Yes, if it's the right time and person, things will fall into place."

"Yes, there is that one person that we click with; we won't have that with anyone else. And that person makes you feel safe, and they accept you for who you are and love you unconditionally."

No, I don't believe in "the one."

"Yeah, the world is huge. And there are billions of people out there. It's a numbers game, and for only one person to be your match is slightly ridiculous when you think of it that way."

"No, but certain people have a connection, and it depends upon time, situation, destiny, and fate."

"There are many different 'fits' depending upon circumstances."

"Some people have 'the one,' but it's manufactured by society. You could miss the other possibilities, who also could be an excellent match."

"Attractions can happen to more than one person, and more than one person can make you feel safe and comfortable."

"No. There is always someone better, but there comes a point when you choose to stay with one person and you work on your relationship."

"There is often 'one' for the moment, and the timing is off for one or both of you. This moment in time is our only time."

"People are capable of recognizing when they have found the right partner in life where there is mutual love, respect, and friendship. When they commit to each other in marriage, they have to continue to work hard."

"Believing in 'the one' and what characteristics 'the one' should have doesn't provide the flexibility and compromise in a relationship."

I think that your opinion of "the one" changes depending upon where you are in your life experience. And maybe, believing in "the one" isn't as realistic as believing in someone—anyone. During an interview, a friend mentioned this saying to me: "Every pot has a lid." I think that this holds true whether you believe in "the one" or not. Everyone can find someone who complements them.

What do I believe? I believe in someone—not necessarily one person for all your life – but for most of it. Someone who can fit the mold in all different aspects. Someone who grows with you.

Thoughts

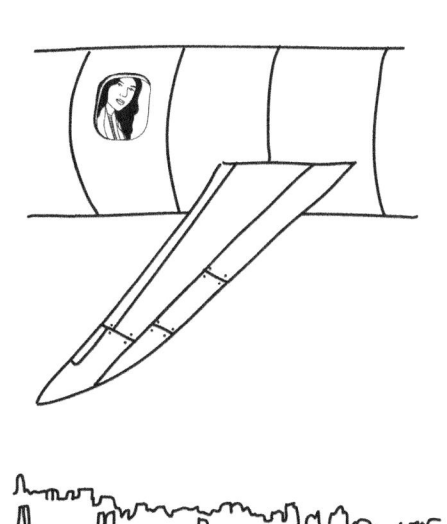

In the end, it really doesn't matter what's on your list because, after all, it's your list. It's personal. It's tailored to you. What really matters is what will make you happy. Truly happy. Not superficially happy. That's lame.

It could be something as simple as the comfort of that first break of morning when the light hits your face and you cuddle with the one you love under a duvet, or something as chaotic as a family reunion at Thanksgiving dinner with secret footsies and romantic glances across the table.

I think sometimes we get so caught up in what other people think and say that we don't pursue what makes us happy. Living in a state of fear and people-pleasing, our lives become not our own but subject to those who control our futures like puppets. The puppet masters can be anyone from overbearing family to know-it-all friends.

So, really, if you take anything from this book, it's that we should all try to live happily and with gusto – and that can be with or without a list.

Whatever will make you happy, and whenever it will, if it makes you happy, it's all good. Because, really, when you leave this life, it's the feelings of those surrounding you that will live on. It won't matter how many boyfriends or girlfriends you have had or if you are married or divorced. What matters is how you live your life.

You cannot control what happens to you, good or bad; you can only control your own reactions to things.

It's just something to think about.

Shout-Outs

Thanks to my family who have provided the basic essentials for daily living for me over the years. I often forget to be thankful for the simple things.

Also, thanks to all my interviewees, who painstakingly answered questions in coffee shops, over the phone, and via e-mail. They are the ones who shared their insightful stories so that I, too, would grow from their experiences.

Sometimes it's hard to recognize the importance of friends until something tragic happens. Friends are important sounding boards. True friends exercise enough patience to run through scenarios ad infinitum. They will stay up and overanalyze with you. They will take walks with you and give you hugs on street corners when you need them. They will be the meeting point for your ex to drop off belongings that were once shared, and they will be the ones who will sporadically send a "Hey. How's it going?" text. They will keep you honest when you don't want to be. And they will be on your side when your feelings are compromised.

I have great girlfriends, new and old. They have helped me so much, each in a unique way. They've comforted me, hugged me, talked with me, listened to me complain, gone shopping with me, watched movies with me, let me plan events, gone on breakfast and lunch dates with me, and gone on trips with me. They've kept me sane and grounded. These ladies are the epitome of support: Cathy C., Alicia M., Jennifer M., Cheryl B., Katie H., and Lisa A.

To my cheering squad, Faye K. and Rita S.—they always turn the negative into a positive and are always there to guide me.

To my go-to editor, for everything from business school applications to freelance creative writing pieces (except this one!), Gina C.—nothing is too big or small for her. She has such a generous heart.

To my friends new and old, Kelly D., Shai M., Sara G., Joyce T., Christina T., Irene S., Leanne C.— you know my potential and don't hold it against me when I act a little crazy.

To the ultimate traveling companions, who have traveled the world with me and still manage to be my friends, Wendy C. and Ruby G.—they have seen me laugh and cry, dance, and sleep in so many time zones.

To my creative, talented spirits who share a great vision—thanks for always wanting to think outside the box. Your talent is amazing: Janelle B., Derek D., Fabrice G., Daniel B., Liz P., Evon A., and Chris N.

To my personal trainer who has kept me healthy (inside and out) and smiling for years, Ayron H. of Wuji Systems (author of *Sanshou Dao: Diary of a Martial Artist*).

And finally to my all-around subject matter experts on the male species. They have heard it all (really, I'm not kidding) and still continue to respond. They give the hug and slap at the same time. Asif P., Simon C., and Kevin A., though we have parted ways for various reasons, I'm sure we will meet again. I miss you all.

I love you all and thank you for being in my life.

REFERENCES

Buss, D. M. *Evolutionary Psychology: The New Science of the Mind*. Needham Heights: Allyn & Bacon, 1999.

Callahan, M. *Are You . . . Ms. Typed?* New York: Crown Publishers, 2009.

DeAngelis, B. *Are You the One for Me?* New York: Random House, 1992.

Gottlieb, L. *Marry Him: The Case for Settling for Mr. Good Enough*. Toronto: Dutton, 2010.

Kearns, J. M. *Shopping for Mr. Right: How to Choose the Right Guy and Get the Most out of Him*. Mississauga: John Wiley & Sons Canada, Ltd., 2011.

Mac, J. *Manslations: Decoding the Secret Language of Men*. Naperville: Sourcebooks, 2009.

McMillan, T. "Why You're Not Married." *The Huffington Post*, February 13, 2011. Retrieved Nov. 23, 2011, from http://www.huffingtonpost.com/tracy-mcmillan/why-youre-not-married_b_822088.html.

Milford, A., and J. Gauvain. *How Not to Marry the Wrong Guy: Is He "The One" or Should You Run?* New York: Broadway Books, 2010.

Noble, M. "The Top 10 Traits That Attract a Man to a Woman." *Your Tango,* May 10, 2011. Retrieved Nov. 23, 2011, from http://www.yourtango.com/201176685/top-10-traits-attract-man-woman.

Reitman, J., and Turner, S. 2009. *Up in the Air.* Paramount Pictures, Cold Spring Pictures and Dreamworks Pictures. Retrieved Nov. 11, 2011, from http://www.imsdb.com/scripts/Up-in-the-Air.html.

Salmahnson, K. *Prince Harming Syndrome.* Long Island City: Langenscheidt Publishing Group, 2009.

Scholfield, S. *Screw Cupid: The Sassy Girls's Guide to Picking Up Hot Guys.* New York: The Experiment, 2009.

Smith, K. "The Top 10 Traits That Attract a Woman to a Man." *Your Tango,* May 11, 2011. Retrieved Nov. 23, 2011, from http://www.yourtango.com/201176681/top-10-traits-attract-woman-man.

Whelan, C. *Marry Smart: The Intelligent Woman's Guide to True Love.* New York: Simon & Schuster Paperbacks, 2009.

Notes

Notes

Notes

Notes

Notes

Notes

Notes

Notes

Notes

Printed in Great Britain
by Amazon